FAREHAM
TO
SALISBURY

Vic Mitchell and Keith Smith

First published September 1989

ISBN 0 906520 67 3

Copyright - Middleton Press, 1989

Design - Deborah Goodridge

Laser typeset by Barbara Mitchell

Published by Middleton Press
          Easebourne Lane
          Midhurst, West Sussex
          GU29 9AZ
          Tel. (0730) 813169

Printed & bound by Biddles Ltd,
          Guildford and Kings Lynn

CONTENTS

ACKNOWLEDGEMENTS

We are very grateful for the help received from many of the photographers mentioned in the credits and also for the assistance received from J. Fairman, D. Pede, R. Randell, E. Staff and N. Stanyon. Tickets have been kindly supplied by G. Croughton, and N. Langridge, Eastleigh goods traffic notes by J. R. W. Kirkby and endless help by our wives.

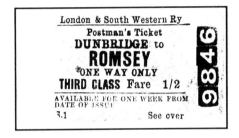

London & South Western Ry
Postman's Ticket
DUNBRIDGE to
ROMSEY
ONE WAY ONLY
THIRD CLASS Fare 1/2
AVAILABLE FOR ONE WEEK FROM
DATE OF ISSUE
3.1   See over
9846

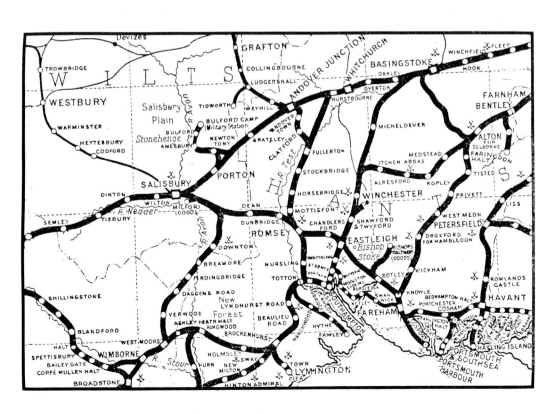

The Southern Railways 1932 map shows the
GWR's routes with narrow lines

GEOGRAPHICAL SETTING

North of Fareham the line tunnels through the sand and clay of the Reading Beds which have caused problems to successive generations of railway engineers. After two miles, the route crosses the River Meon and, just beyond Botley, it passes over the River Hamble.

Apart from the Brickearth and Alluvium in the valleys, the railway passes over the sand and clay of the Bracklesham Beds as far as Romsey, crosses the Itchen Valley near Eastleigh and runs for three miles beside the River Test north of Romsey. Thereafter it enters the valley of the River Dun and traverses Chalk to West Grimstead. This material has given rise to some railway traffic which is detailed elsewhere in this volume.

The route continues up the valley until reaching the Alderbury area, where it passes over an extension of the sandy Bagshot Beds and then skirts the eastern flank of the Avon Valley before descending into the Bourne Valley.

Salisbury is situated at the confluence of the Rivers Nadder, Bourne and Avon, the latter entering the sea at Christchurch. The city is surrounded by the Chalk of Salisbury Plain, a projection of which the railway passes through, by means of a tunnel, to reach the present station.

HISTORICAL BACKGROUND

The line between Winchester and Southampton came into use on 10th June 1839, but the route to London was not complete until May 1840. On 29th November 1841 the branch to Gosport was opened, the junction being at Bishopstoke (known as Eastleigh from 1889). After being in use for only four days, the branch was closed until 7th February 1842, owing to serious land instability north of Fareham.

A branch from Bishopstoke to Salisbury (Milford) was opened to goods traffic on 27th January 1847 and to passengers on 9th March of that year. The junction was arranged for through running to Southampton, as it was considered that most traffic would be destined for there and not London. In the autumn of 1848, the line from Fareham to Portsmouth via Cosham was brought into use.

The GWR's broad gauge tracks arrived at Salisbury (Fisherton) in 1856 and from 1st May 1857 the London & South Western Railway commenced direct services from London via Basingstoke. Initially these trains used the Milford terminus, which involved reversal.

Services were extended west from Salisbury to Gillingham on 2nd May 1859, after which date the Milford station ceased to be used for passengers.

Traffic on the short branch from Botley to Bishops Waltham commenced on 1st June 1863.

Part of the route in the Romsey area was used by trains from the new Andover-Redbridge line from 6th March 1865. Additional trains over the western end of the route commenced on 20th December 1866, when the line to West Moors came into use.

Fareham became a more important junction on 2nd September 1889 when a single line from Netley was completed. This formed part of a direct route to Southampton.

The final development in the area took place on 1st June 1903 when the Meon Valley services to Alton commenced to operate between Fareham and Knowle Junction.

Withdrawal of passenger services took place as follows -
2nd January 1933 Botley-Bishops Waltham
8th June 1953 Fareham-Gosport
5th February 1955 Fareham-Alton
6th May 1964 Salisbury-West Moors
7th September 1964 Romsey-Andover
5th May 1969 Romsey-Eastleigh

Notable changes in traction have been the introduction of diesel-electric units for local services in 1957 and the elimination of steam haulage in 1967. In 1988, work commenced on a £16.4m electrification scheme to cover the lines radiating from Fareham to Eastleigh, St. Denys and Portsmouth, with completion scheduled for May 1990.

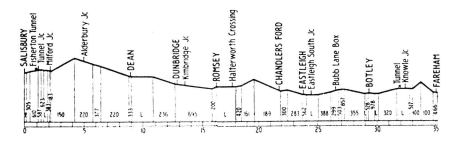

PASSENGER SERVICES

Initially there were six return journeys on the Gosport and Salisbury branches but for most of the 19th century eight trains were provided on weekdays, with three on Sundays.

Through services between Portsmouth and Bristol or Cardiff commenced in 1892 but gradually an increasing proportion of these were routed via Southampton instead of Eastleigh.

The 1906 timetable showed fifteen trains on weekdays on most of the route, with less than half that on Sundays. Between 1863 and 1915 the Fareham route carried passengers for the Isle of Wight travelling via Stokes Bay. For a short period there were through coaches from the Midlands.

Until the advent of dieselisation in 1957, the pattern of services was complex in terms of the destinations served and irregular in time intervals. This is well illustrated by the up weekday departures from Chandlers Ford in August 1934.

am
7.04 Fareham
8.10 Southampton Terminus
8.39 Portsmouth Harbour
9.31 Southampton West
10.27 Portsmouth & Southsea
11.41 Southampton Terminus
pm
12.18 Eastleigh
1.35 Eastleigh (Portsmouth & Southsea
on Saturdays)

2.08 Southampton Terminus
3.06 Ditto
5.02 Southampton West
6.07 Southampton Terminus (through
from Reading)
7.09 Portsmouth & Southsea
7.36 Southampton West
8.27 Southampton Terminus
9.03 Portsmouth & Southsea
9.28 Ditto
10.12 Southampton Terminus

The diesel operated services have been on a regular hourly interval basis and the last link with the old timetable was severed in May 1989, when the Bristol - Southampton mail ceased to run via Eastleigh.

Bishops Waltham Branch

The initial timetable showed six weekday and three Sunday trains but, by 1869, this had been reduced to four on weekdays only. From 1889, there were seven journeys and, with the introduction of railmotors in 1907, this was increased to twelve. Sunday trains were reintroduced at this time, with six or seven trips being provided until 1918 and then four until 1931, when they were withdrawn permanently. By 1925, the weekday service had been reduced to nine journeys and in the final years, it was further trimmed to only six.

	BOTLEY and BISHOP'S WALTHAM.—Southern.													
Miles		Week Days.										Sundays.		
		mrn	mrn	mrn	aft	aft	aft	aft	aft	aft		mrn	aft	aft	aft
	Botley .... dep.	8 20	9 25	1055	1215	2 20	3 40	4 56	6 58	0		8 10	5 40	6 25	8 0
	Durley Halt	8 24	9 29	11 1	1219	2 24	3 44	5 0	6 128	4		8 14	5 44	6 29	8 4
3½	Bishop's Waltham ...... arr.	8 30	9 35	1110	1225	2 30	3 50	5 ·	6 188	10		8 20	5 50	6 35	8 10
Miles		Week Days.										Sundays.		
		mrn	mrn	mrn	mrn	aft	aft	aft	aft	aft		mrn	aft	aft	aft
	Bishop's Waltham ... dep.	7 50	9 0	10 5	1140	1 35	3 5	4 35	5 22	7 15		8 30	5 15	6 07	30
	Durley Halt	7 56	9 6	1011	1146	1 41	3 11	4 41	5 28	7 21		8 36	5 21	6 7	36
3½	Botley 170, 174 .... arr.	8 0	9 10	1015	1150	1 45	3 15	4 45	5 32	7 25		8 40	5 25	6 10	7 40

1925

All maps are to the scale of 25" to 1 mile, unless otherwise stated.

FAREHAM

1. The main building (right) dates from the opening of the line to Gosport in 1841, while the island platform (left) was created in 1888- 89, when the station was enlarged to handle the trains on the new line from Netley. (Lens of Sutton)

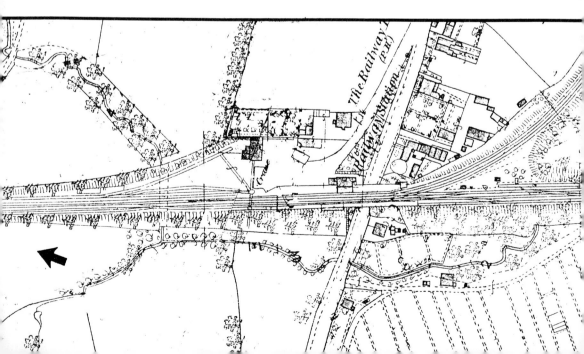

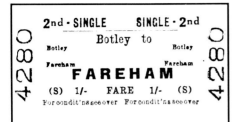

The first edition shows the arrangement before the Netley line was opened. The Eastleigh - Gosport route runs from left to right. Land for additional sidings on both sides of the track was purchased in May 1898.

2. The difference between the earlier and later canopies is evident as class M7 no. E38 waits in the down platform in August 1930. The Southern Railway's prefix letters on former LSWR engines were dropped in the following July. (D. Cullum coll.)

3. Class C8 no. 299 approaches the down platform on 8th September 1931, with a train from the GWR destined for Portsmouth & Southsea. Part of the 10 ton capacity portal crane is visible, beyond the goods vans which are being shunted by class A12 0-4-2 no.601. (D. Cullum coll.)

4. On the left, class T9 4-4-0 no. 30301 calls at platform 3 with the 11.15 Portsmouth & Southsea to Bristol (Temple Meads) service. On the right, class 2MT no. 41317 waits with the 11.45 departure for Andover Junction, via Southampton Central. It had arrived at 11.26 from Portsmouth and had reversed onto the Gosport branch to reach platform 4, a regular procedure on Saturdays. Extreme right is 700 class 0-6-0 no. 30316. (D. Fereday Glenn)

London & South Western Ry.
This Ticket is issued subject to the By-laws Regulations & Conditions stated in the Company's Time Tables Bills & Notices.
BOTLEY to
EASTLEIGH
Botley   Botley
Eastleigh   Eastleigh
3rd CLASS   3rd CLASS
Fare 5½d   Fare 5½d

3029   3029

5. The signalman from East Box extends his arm to collect the single line tablet, as class 5 no. 73043 arrives with a parcels train from Eastleigh on 13th March 1965. Tracks diverge in the foreground to Southampton and in the background to the "tunnel avoiding lines" on the Eastleigh route. (E. Wilmshurst)

6. The 17.20 all stations Eastleigh to Fratton service was headed by class 4 2-6-4T no. 80151 on 29th March 1967. The stone building remains in use but the distinctive coupled chimneys have been lost, as has the footbridge roofing, although half of the latter was replaced in 1988. (J. Scrace)

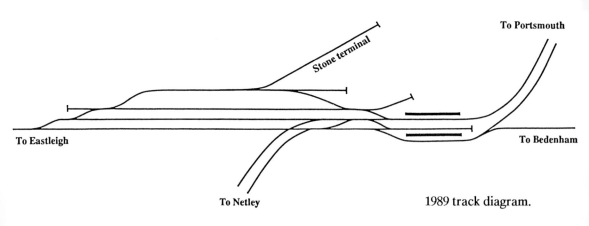

To Portsmouth

Stone terminal

To Eastleigh

To Bedenham

To Netley

1989 track diagram.

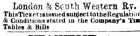

PASSENGERS
MUST NOT CROSS
THE LINE HERE

7. Due to engineering works at Cosham on 5th October 1969, trains terminated at Fareham and an Eastleigh service is seen departing from the former Meon Valley bay, the "A" indicating the Alton route. East Box can be seen at the west end of the station - "East" meaning that it was nearest to Waterloo, which was at the eastern end of the LSWR. (J. H. Bird)

London & South Western Ry.
This Ticket is issued subject to the Regulations
& Conditions stated in the Company's Time
Tables & Bills

SWANWICK to
FAREHAM

Swanwick	Swanwick
Fareham	Fareham
3rd CLASS	3rd CLASS
Fare 4d	Fare 4d

653   653

8. Semaphore signalling remained in use until 20th June 1982 when control of the area was transferred to Eastleigh Panel Box. No. D1036 *Western Emperor* is seen on 22nd July 1970, having worked a train to the new stone terminal. The goods shed in the background was closed in the previous month and was demolished in the summer of 1987. (J. Scrace)

lower left

9. A class 33 diesel with Mk. 1 coaches represents a typical Cardiff - Portsmouth Harbour train until the introduction of Sprinters in May 1988. No. 33026 is passing the roadstone terminal on 26th January 1984. The nearer two sidings were removed in 1989 but Mendip limestone still arrived in 1380 tonne ARC block trains from Whatley, five times per week. Discharge time is two and a half hours. (M. Turvey)

10. On 28th July 1988, the Minister of Transport descended steps from platform 3 and screwed down a "golden pot" to inaugurate work on the Solent area electrification scheme. The officials had arrived in Wessex Electric unit no. 2413 which was propelled from Southampton by no. 33114 *Sultan*. (M. Turvey)

11. A DEMU is about to obscure the remaining part of the Gosport branch as it arrives on 1st October 1988, bound for Reading. On 10th March 1968 the tracks were slewed to allow trains from Portsmouth to run over a new bridge span into platform 4. There is now no platform no. 1. The new bridges were required to permit road widening. (A. C. Mott)

12. The division and joining of trains at Fareham ceased with the end of steam but recommenced with the introduction of Sprinters in May 1988. Two coaches from Brighton are being coupled to two from Portsmouth Harbour at 9.31 on 24th January 1989. The class 156 units had been intended for use in Scotland but were introduced onto the Cardiff services in December 1987, owing to door control problems on the class 155. (V. Mitchell)

Other photographs of this station can be seen in our *Branch Lines to Alton* and *Portsmouth to Southampton* albums and in Peter Hay's *Steaming through East Hants*.

NORTH OF FAREHAM

13. The headshunt of the goods yard is behind the train from Alton, which was being propelled by class M7 no. 30480 on 24th June 1950. One or both of the lines in the foreground were in use from 1906 until 1973. They avoided the tunnels and climbed steeply over the high ground to the west of them. (D. Cullum)

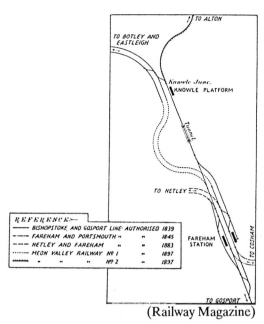

(Railway Magazine)

14. The original single tunnel collapsed soon after opening and a short length of cutting was substituted. Heavy mobile clay has subsequently caused many stability problems, hence the need for a diversionary route, which was opened in 1904 as a single line. This is a 1955 northward view from the 553 yd. no. 2 tunnel, looking over the 56 yd. no. 1 tunnel, above which the M27 now passes. A diagram in *Branch Lines to Alton* shows the complex evolution of lines in this area. (D. Cullum)

15. Fontley Abattoir siding was on the west side of the line and is seen in 1955. It had been laid two years earlier for the Ministry of Food and was usable until January 1970. It was situated beyond the bridge which is barely visible in the background of the previous photograph. Fontley Brickworks siding, between the bridge and the tunnel, was in use until 1962. (D. Cullum)

KNOWLE HALT

16. The following five photographs are in geographical order, from the south. The double track of the diversion converged upon the single line of the original route under a footbridge, but there was no connection between them for over half a mile. (D. Cullum)

17. The halt is seen from the road bridge that is featured in the previous picture. The LCGB railtour is running from Droxford to Gosport on 30th April 1961, hauled by ex-LBSCR class E1 0-6-0T no. 32694 and piloted by ex LSWR class O2 0-4-4T no. 30200. (S. C. Nash)

18. Opened as Knowle Asylum Halt on 1st May 1907, the single platform was located on the tunnel route. The hospital's gasworks is visible beyond the gate to the private siding, which could hold up to 15 wagons. Known simply as Knowle Halt after 1942, the platform was last used on 4th April 1964, but was still visible in 1989. (D. Cullum)

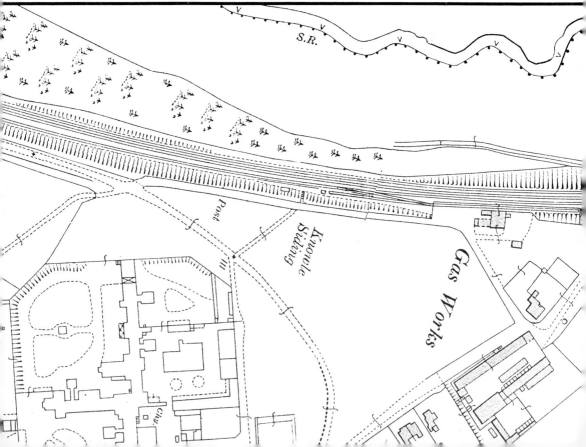

S.R.

Post

Knowle Siding

Gas Works

19. Knowle Hospital and its siding were both opened in 1853. Initially there were 600 patients, the number soon increasing to about 2000. The siding was mainly used for coal for heating the hospital, the boilerhouse chimney being visible near the centre of the complex. The gasworks did not require any coal as it produced acetylene for lighting the hospital. The halt was used by staff and visitors, tickets being available from the hospital porter's lodge. The line from Fareham is at the top of the picture, the halt being obscured by the trees on the right. (P. Keat coll.)

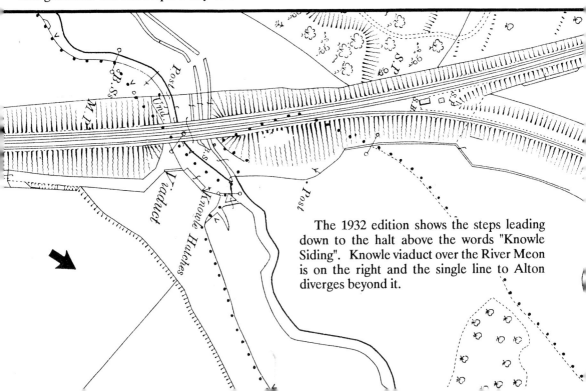

The 1932 edition shows the steps leading down to the halt above the words "Knowle Siding". Knowle viaduct over the River Meon is on the right and the single line to Alton diverges beyond it.

20. DEMU no. 1101 runs from Eastleigh to Portsmouth on 9th March 1961 and passes the Knowle siding, which was closed on 10th December 1962. The parapets of the viaduct over the River Meon are in the distance. (L. Elsey)

ALTON, WEST MEON, and FAREHAM.—London and South Western.												
Miles.	**Down.**	**Week Days.**					**Sundays.**		Miles.	**Up.**	**Week Days.**					**Sundays.**	
	Waterloo Station.	mrn	mrn	aft	aft	aft	aft	mrn	aft			Fareham	mrn	mrn	aft	aft	aft	aft	mrn	aft
	146 London........dep.	7 10	9 15	1 45	4 10	5 30		6 10			2	Knowle Platform........	7 30	10 11	3 74	3 97	4 09	5 92	7 49	6 45
	Alton........dep.	8 57	11 55	3 15	5 31	7 15			8 1		4½	Wickham	7 33	10 11	4 64	3 97	5 8	9 10	7 58	6 50
5¼	Tisted §§	9 3	12 6	3 26	6 2	7 25			8 12		9¼	Droxford ††	7 50	11 56	4 93	9 1	9 18		8 87	6
8½	Privett	9 15	12 13	3 36	6 9	7 34			8 19		12¾	West Meon	7 55	11 9	2 44	4 58	8 17		8 15	7 14
12½	West Meon	8 23	12 22	3 40	6 16	7 42	1 43	8 24	8 26		17½	Privett	8 9	11 9	2 14	5 86	8 27		8	7 25
16½	Droxford ††	9 30	12 27	3 47	6 23	7 49		8 31	8 33		20½	Tisted §§	8 15	11 25	2 30	5 14	8 33		8	7 32
21¼	Wickham	9 39	12 35	3 56	6 21	7 57	19 19	8 40	8 41		23½	Alton 146, 147, 148 arr.	8 29	11 32	2 35	5 22	8 41		8	7 40
23½	Knowle Platform........	9 44	12 40		6 26	8					72¼	147 London (W'loo) arr.	10 12	1 24	4 36	7 23	10 42			9 42
25¼	Fareham 152, 154...arr.	9 48	12 44	3 6	6 40	8 5	10 19		8 48	8 49										

d Leaves at 1 10 a'ft. on Saturdays.	h Stops on Thursdays ; also on the last	s Stops on Saturdays only.	†† Station for Hambledon (3 miles).
‡ Stops on Thursdays and Saturdays.	Wednesday in the month.		§§ Station for Selborne (2½ miles).

The 1917 timetable.

21. Knowle signal box was at the junction with the Meon Valley line, which is seen in the foreground in 1952. The box also controlled the junction of the tunnel avoiding lines with the direct route. The box was closed on 6th May 1973 when the rest of the route to Botley was singled. (D. Cullum)

BOTLEY

22. The station opened with the line. The approach road fell gently down from the main road to the goods yard but the access to the up platform and booking office was at the top of the slope, through a rectangular archway and down a flight of stairs. The down platform could be reached via the footbridge, a pathway leading to this on the level, through a gate situated just off the right of the picture. (Lens of Sutton)

23. For about three weeks each year, strawberries were despatched in vast quantities. For example, in 1906, 1013 tons were loaded, with as many as 30,000 baskets being transferred to 60 vans in a day. This view is prior to 1911, when the left arch of the bridge was replaced with a steel span to permit lengthening of the head shunt. (Lens of Sutton)

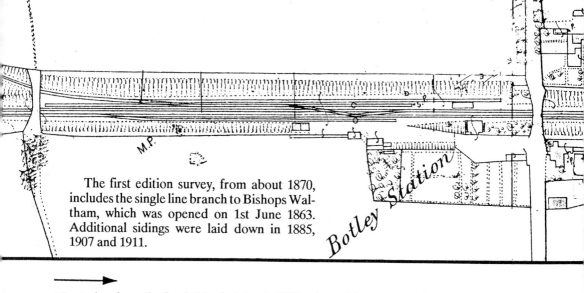

The first edition survey, from about 1870, includes the single line branch to Bishops Waltham, which was opened on 1st June 1863. Additional sidings were laid down in 1885, 1907 and 1911.

Botley Station

25. A view from the footbridge in March 1968 shows the Bishops Waltham branch curving away under the brick arch. On the right is the branch bay, last used regularly on 31st December 1932 - there were only two passengers on the last train! (J. Scrace)

24. Class L12 no. 30426 is shunting vans on 29th June 1950. By that time, strawberry traffic had diminished to about 15 van loads in the season, mainly due to a plant disease in the locality. Goods inward included coal and fertiliser and had earlier included straw and dung for the soft fruit growers. (D. Cullum)

26. DEMU no. 1103 forms the 15.03 Portsmouth & Southsea to Romsey service, part of a regular hourly timetable. Staffing ceased on 14th July 1968, four months after this photograph was taken. The Railway Hotel is in the background. (J. Scrace)

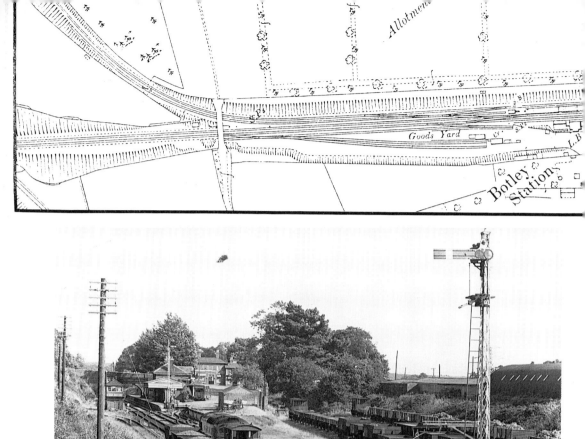

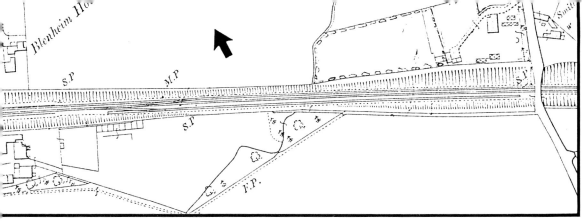

The 1909 survey at 20" to 1 mile, shows the position of the 2-ton crane (Cr.) and that a siding had been laid beside the branch line. A refuge siding, east of the station, was added in 1894. Beyond it is Tapnage Tunnel, which is 122 yds. long.

27. The goods yard closed on 2nd October 1967 but the tracks were retained until 1971. This is the scene in August 1968 during major track relaying operations. Freight services on the Bishops Waltham branch were operated until 27th April 1962, most of the track being lifted in 1963. (J. H. Bird)

28. On 19th November 1972, the first half mile of the branch was brought back into use to serve a new stone terminal for Foster Yeoman. Nos. 37213 and 37254 are seen hauling wagons slowly over the discharge pit on 26th March 1983. The signal box ceased to be a block post on 20th June 1982 but was retained to control the crossover during the running round of stone trains. On the left, conveyors pass over the main line to transfer the stone to a tarmac coating plant, which was built in part of the former goods yard. (J. Petley)

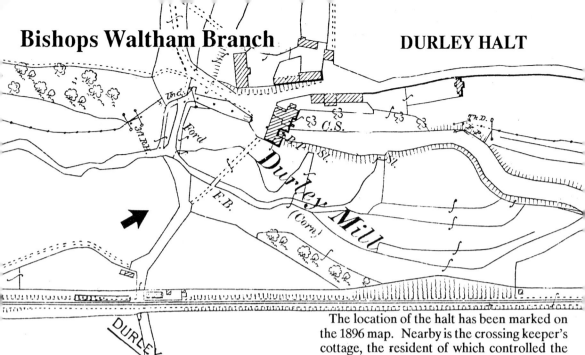

The location of the halt has been marked on the 1896 map. Nearby is the crossing keeper's cottage, the resident of which controlled the gates until April 1954.

29. Nothing remained of the little used halt when the first passenger carrying train for nearly twenty years passed by on 14th June 1952. The RCTS special was hauled by a class C14 0-4-0T, the locomotive being even shorter than the Steam Motor Car referred to in the opening notice and illustrated in picture no. 31. (L. Elsey)

LONDON & SOUTH WESTERN RAILWAY.

Instructions to District Superintendents, Station Masters, Inspectors, Enginemen, Guards, Signalmen, and all others concerned, as to the

Opening of a new Halt, to be known as

"DURLEY HALT,"

BETWEEN

BOTLEY AND BISHOP'S WALTHAM STATIONS,

On THURSDAY, 23rd DECEMBER, 1909.

A new Halt, to be known as "Durley Halt," has been provided at Durley Mill Level Crossing, situated 1 mile 30 chains from Botley Station and 2 miles 30 chains from Bishop's Waltham Station, and on and from Thursday, 23rd December, the Steam Motor Car working between Botley and Bishop's Waltham will call at the Halt to take up and set down Passengers.

A platform, 120 feet in length, situated on the down side of the single line, has been provided, but there will be no staff, signals or waiting room accommodation.

The new Halt will come under the supervision of the Station Master at Bishop's Waltham, who must make frequent inspections of it and see that everything is in order, and he must also arrange for the lighting and extinguishing of the lamps when required.

The Guard, accompanying the Motor Car, will issue Tickets, which must be punched by the Bell-punch, to all Passengers joining the Car at the Halt. He must pay in his money daily to the Station Master at Bishop's Waltham, who will remit it in the usual way.

When an ordinary coach is attached to the Motor Car as a trailer, the Passengers joining at the Halt must, if there be room, ride in the Motor Car in order that Tickets may be issued to them.

Tickets held by Passengers in the Motor Car must be examined by the Guard, and the Tickets of Passengers alighting at the Halt must be collected by him.

HENRY HOLMES,
Superintendent of the Line.

WATERLOO STATION,
    22nd December, 1909.
    (V. 24,116.)

Waterlow & Sons Limited, Printers, London Wall, London.

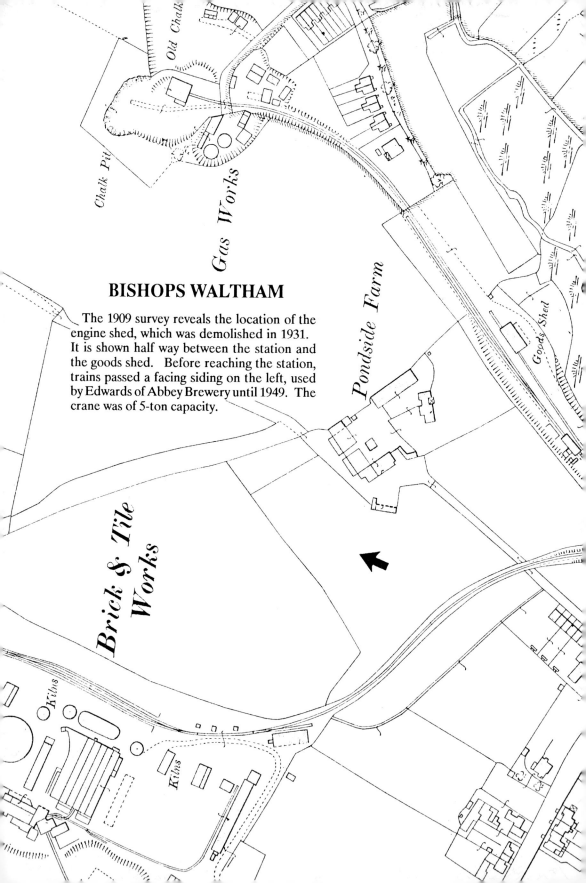

BISHOPS WALTHAM

The 1909 survey reveals the location of the engine shed, which was demolished in 1931. It is shown half way between the station and the goods shed. Before reaching the station, trains passed a facing siding on the left, used by Edwards of Abbey Brewery until 1949. The crane was of 5-ton capacity.

Chalk Pit

Old Chalk

Gas Works

Pondside Farm

Goods Shed

Brick & Tile Works

Kilns

Kilns

Grammar School

P.H.

Smy.

HIGH

St GEORGE'S SQUARE

Bank

Crown
Inn

P.H.

Eastway

Tower

Wall

Fire
Engine Station

Moat

Lodge
(Rems.of)

Moat

OFFICE

Palace
(Ruins of)

Great Hall

Court

Court

Inner

Court

Tower

Palace House

Bishop's

Station

Bishop's Waltham Pond

S.P.

S.P.

S.P.

S.B.

St.

117

M.S

Gosport 13

Abbey Mill
(Corn)

Pond
(Site of)

Tower

RIA ROAD

MARTIN'S STREET

Gravel Pit

30.   Open to passengers from 1st June 1863 until 30th December 1932, the station is seen from Victoria Road, early this century.   For almost all of the first two years of the line, a temporary station was in use, south of the level crossing. (Lens of Sutton)

31.   From 1905 until about 1915, passengers were carried by steam railcar.   The siding curving away on the left led to Blanchard's Brick & Tile Works, which was in production until 1956 although rail traffic had ceased more than a decade earlier. (Lens of Sutton)

32. A photograph from about 1914 includes the signal box, which had 16 levers and a gate wheel. It was closed on 6th December 1935, after which date most signals were removed and the gates were worked by hand. (Lens of Sutton)

33. Nationalisation in 1948 had little impact on the local railway scene, except that by 1953 the van was endorsed *BRITISH ROAD SERVICES RAILWAY CARTAGE*. The red and yellow brickwork was contained within timber framing, a technique employed to reduce the weight of the building on the clay subsoil which has poor load bearing properties. (J. H. Aston)

34. The second railway enthusiasts' special to visit the branch was operated by the Stephenson Locomotive Society on 3rd May 1953 and was composed of two push-pull sets with class M7 no. 30110 in the middle. It ran beyond the station to the goods shed. (S. C. Nash)

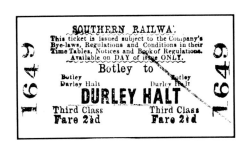

SOUTHERN RAILWAY.
This ticket is issued subject to the Company's Bye-laws, Regulations and Conditions in their Time Tables, Notices and Book of Regulations.
Available on DAY of issue ONLY.
Botley   to
Botley   Botley
Durley Halt   Durley Halt
DURLEY HALT
Third Class   Third Class
Fare 2½d   Fare 2½d

1649   1649

35. Local residents appeared that day to witness the event. The third and final special was a two coach train organised by the Branch Line Society on 7th March 1959 and hauled by class M7 no. 30111. (C. L. Caddy coll.)

36. A 1962 photograph shows the overlapping gates and that the canopy had been lost. The entire building was demolished a little later, to make way for a roundabout and a relief road. The sign still proclaimed "S.R." The gates were retained to form a feature at the new roundabout. (R. M. Casserley)

37. Bubb Lane signal box was in use until 12th December 1952 and was photographed in June 1950, by which time the signal post had developed a severe tilt.   Also on the down side, there were extensive sidings for an Admiralty Depot, which were in use from 1952 until 1966. To the south, a new station for Hedge End is planned, to be opened in May 1990. (D. Cullum)

38.   The 8.53am Eastleigh to Portsmouth &
Southsea on 23rd March 1957 was hauled by
LMS designed 2-6-4T no. 42080 and is seen
running past the locomotive works.   The line
in the foreground linked the carriage works
with the carriage sidings.   (L. Elsey)

39.   With the locomotive works and Eastleigh
South Box on the left, 6-car DEMU no. 1001
makes its first run, working the 10.17am from
Eastleigh to Fareham on 17th January 1957.
The flat body sides were necessary for use in
the small tunnels on the Tonbridge - Hastings
line.   (L. Elsey)

41. In the distance is the single line which curves into the station. This section was singled on 31st March 1978. On the right is the Byrail aggregate depot, which opened in July 1979, and by 1989 was receiving half a million tonnes of limestone from Merehead. The train is being handled by one of Foster Yeoman's five class 59 General Motors diesels. Beyond are the private sidings of H. Young and Silcock & Collings, road vehicle transporters, seldom used when photographed in January 1989. (V. Mitchell)

←

40. Eastleigh South Box was in use until 6th November 1966 when the new Eastleigh Panel was commissioned. It was a block post and also controlled access to the carriage works and the southern approaches to the locomotive works and running shed. (L. Elsey)

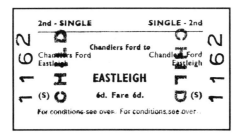

2nd - SINGLE   SINGLE - 2nd

Chandlers Ford to

Chandlers Ford   Chandlers Ford
Eastleigh   Eastleigh

EASTLEIGH

(S)   6d. Fare 6d.   (S)

For conditions see over. For conditions see over.

EASTLEIGH LOCOMOTIVE WORKS

42. Following the successful relocation of the LSWR carriage and wagon works from London in 1891, locomotive building was transferred from the cramped premises at Nine Elms in 1909. On the left are the stores and paint shop, behind which the coppersmiths, axle shop and power house are located. In the distance are the forge and brass foundry, the chimney projecting above the main shops being that of the iron foundry.
(National Railway Museum)

43. The works was laid out to minimise
material handling and overhead travelling
cranes were provided for the movement of
components. Beyond the heap of ashpans is

Adams radial 4-4-2T no. 58, which was withdrawn in 1925, having been used in its final years on the Wimbledon - Ludgate Hill motor train service. (National Railway Museum)

44. When completed the works comprised four main sections, the Fareham line being seen to the left of them. On the right is the office block; next to it are the double tracks from the running shed and point rodding separates them from the main line to Southampton. The line in the foreground was known as the "Dorset siding" and was disconnected in 1989. (Lens of Sutton)

45. Dugald Drummond was mechanical engineer from 1895 until 1912 and in 1899 he built this unique 4-2-4 to convey him between Nine Elms and his home at Surbiton. He was responsible for the move of the works to Eastleigh which resulted in him having a longer daily journey. It did, however, give him greater opportunity to pass comments directly to drivers of trains on the quadruple track section of his trip, as he raced past in his speedy combination. "The Bug" was dismantled during WWII but the body survived and is to be found at the Hampshire Narrow Gauge Railway, near Durley. (S. W. Baker)

46. The works was heavily involved in varied non-railway work during WWII, such as the manufacture of landing craft. This 1949 view shows the engine dump and stocks of timber and coal. (Lens of Sutton)

47. Stored out of use on 28th August 1954 were class O458 Hawthorn Leslie 0-4-0ST *Ironside* (once the Guildford pilot engine), Terrier *Boxhill* and class T3 no. 563, both now at the National Railway Museum. (T. Wright)

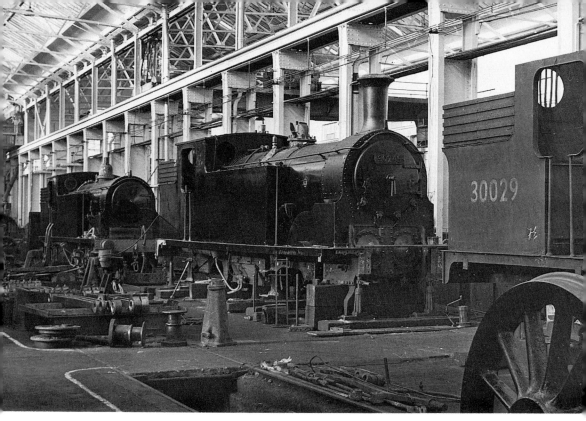

48.   On 27th February 1960, three M7s were being overhauled, the middle one being no. 30245, which was later acquired by the National Railway Museum and more recently has been on loan to the Mid-Hants Railway. (T. Wright)

EASTLEIGH SHED

49. Eastleigh's third and largest running shed was in use from 1903 until 1967 and is seen with a fifth 3-road bay under construction on the right. The lamp is a Jablachcoff candle, an early form of self adjusting arc light.
(J. R. W. Kirkby coll.)

50. Another view of the south end of the shed includes class X2 no. 590 on the right. As this engine was withdrawn in 1937, it helps to date the photograph. As many as 120 locomotives at one time were allocated here in the shed's heyday. (J. R. W. Kirkby coll.)

51. Two rows of staff dwellings were built between the running shed and the works, one of them partly visible in August 1958 as no. 34028 *Eddystone* takes on fuel direct from the coal stack. The elevated coal stage is behind the crane. (T. Wright)

52. An inclined siding allowed wagons to be propelled into the coal stage where coal was transferred in wheeled tubs to the tenders. The 20,000 gallon water tank dominates the scene on 18th May 1963, the last day that BR steamed a Schools class. The last survivor was no. 30934 *St. Lawrence.* (E. Wilmshurst)

53. A diesel depot was established in 1962, south of the coaling stage, and access was provided at both ends. By 1979, the depot had eight roads and there were carriage berthing sidings both sides of it - seven to the east and fifteen to the west. (M. Turvey)

EASTLEIGH

54. Recent researches have revealed that the station did not come into use when the main line was opened, but that the nearest station was at Twyford, over three miles to the north. The station was opened with the Gosport branch, on 29th November 1841 and was named "Bishopstoke", the suffix "Junction" being added in December 1852. The station was renamed "Eastleigh & Bishopstoke" in July 1889, "Bishopstoke" being dropped on 9th July 1923. The new entrance and covered footbridge were built when the up loop line was added in 1875. The coupled chimneys on the now demolished Junction Hotel (centre) were similar to those on the original station building. (Lens of Sutton)

55. The signal gantry on the left spans the Fareham lines and to the right of it is the second running shed. Eastleigh West Box is partly obscured by the rear locomotive on the right, as gangs dig out the points on 25th April 1908. In the down loop is 460 class 4-4-0 no. 460. (Lens of Sutton)

56.   Class L11 no. 439 gleams brightly as she prepares to take the curve to Portsmouth with a train from the GWR at Basingstoke on 30th July 1939.   The large East Box is visible beyond the road bridge. (H. C. Casserley)

The 1913 Tourist Map at 1" to 1 mile emphasises the formal layout of the modern railway town of Eastleigh, when compared with the casual plan of nearby Bishopstoke.

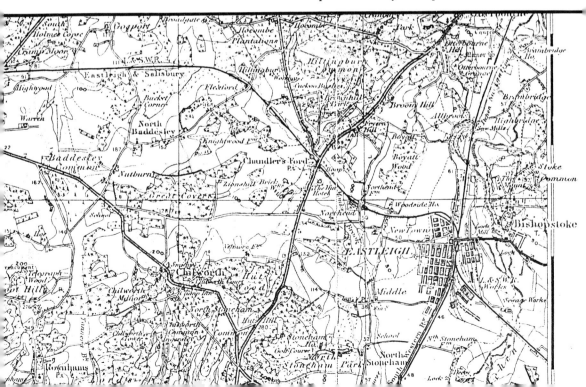

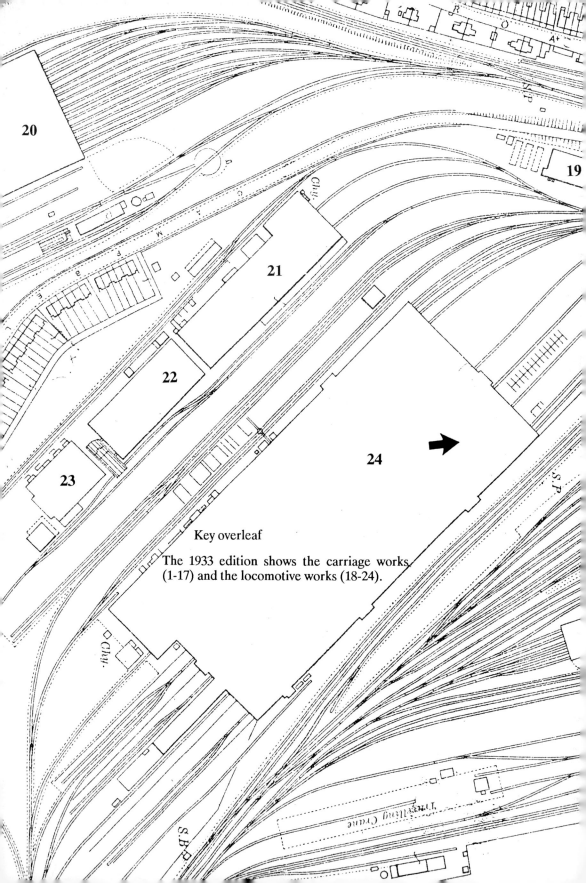

20

19

21

22

23

24

Chy.

Chy.

S.P.

S.B.

S.B.

Travelling Crane

Key overleaf

The 1933 edition shows the carriage works
(1-17) and the locomotive works (18-24).

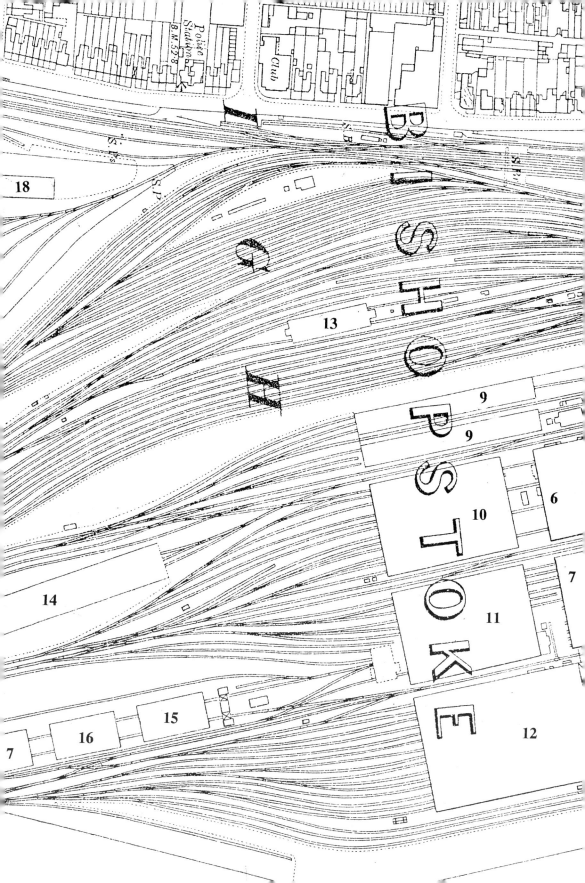

Club

Church
of the
resurrection

Regal
Theatre

Bank
Bank

Club

Club

Club

P.H.

P.H.
Hotel

P.H.

G.P
S. Br

L.B.
Bank

Cr

Goods
Shed

Cr

S.B.

Station

Cattle
Pens

Capstan

Cr

1

4

5

6

2

3

7

8

L.B.

L.B.

BARTON ROAD

ROAD

B
I
S

S
+H
C P

Barton

Urinal

Students
(Corn)

Barton Mill (Corn)

Secondary
School

Barton

Allo
Gard

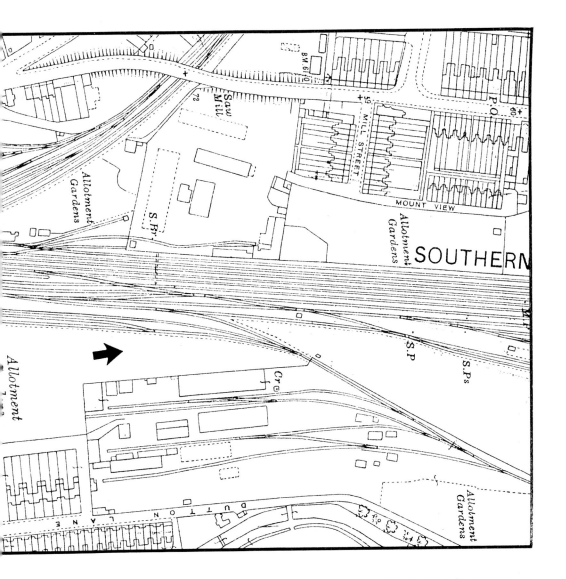

1	Store	15-17	Timber Sheds
2-3	Paint Shops	18	General Offices
4	Tinsmith's Shop	19	Dining Hall
5	Electric Power House	20	Loco Running Shed
6	Machine and Smith's Shop	21	Brass Foundry
7	Body Shop		Iron Foundry
8	Wagon Shop		Pattern Shop
9	Stores	22	Firebrick Shed
10	Lifting Shop		Stores
11	Saw Mill	23	Forge
12	Wagon Shop	24	Erecting, Fitting,
13	Tranship Shed		Paint, Machine,
14	Stock Shed		Smiths and Brass Shops

57.   A view north from West Box reveals the
sinuous course of the up loop which remained
in use until January 1981.   The low buildings
with pitched roofs on the down island platform
were demolished in 1967.
(Lens of Sutton)

58.   Electrification of the London - Bournemouth line took place in 1967, an up stopping
EMU being visible behind the rear coach of
the DEMU seen departing for Romsey.   The
10 ton portal crane of the Town Yard was
photographed from the Panel Box in 1968.
Freight facilities were withdrawn on 11th
October 1977.   (J. H. Bird)

59. A 1976 photograph of the entrance emphasises the restricted access for road vehicles. Thirteen years later a refurbishment scheme was started which included the demolition of these buildings and provision of direct access to the up platform once again. The canopy is over the entrance for parcels. (J. Scrace)

60. An unusual feature of platform 2 was the swing bridge which linked it with the parcels office. Although it carried warning lamps, its movement was interlocked with the signalling system. A similar bridge was still to be found in use at Brockenhurst in 1989. (J. Scrace)

61. D1058 *Western Nobleman* creeps through platform 2 on 25th June 1976 with empty stone wagons from Fareham to Westbury. The white building dates from the 1840s and has the fenestrated chimney stacks characteristic of the contemporary stations at Romsey, Fareham, Gosport and Southampton. (J. Scrace)

62. On 26th July 1976, the 8.28 Westbury to Botley stone train was hauled by no. D1009 *Western Invader*. As it snakes round the 20

63. No. 47125 roars along the up through line with the 8.50 Weymouth to Sheffield on 26th July 1976, while no. 33016 waits at platform 3. Platform 4 was by then signalled for reversible running and the canopy had been reduced. (J. Scrace)

chain curve, it passes the Panel Box which superseded the East, West and South Boxes on 6th November 1966. (J. Scrace)

64. DEMU no. 1125 formed the 15.57 from Portsmouth Harbour on 14th May 1987 and is seen passing the Marshalling and Tipton Yards. These ceased to be used in May 1982 but were retained for stock storage. The Fareham line runs alongsde the BREL works in the background. (J. Scrace)

65. An ugly featureless block was erected in 1967 to accommodate staff messrooms and offices, together with a passenger buffet. The 14.42 Waterloo to Bournemouth stopping train waits on 14th May 1981 and in the back-ground are the buildings of the carriage works, which closed in 1968. Many of these now form part of the Barton & Tower Industrial Estates. (J. Scrace)

A continuation of the previous map shows the private siding of the bacon factory. It was laid down in 1924 for the Hampshire Farmers' Cooperative and closed in 1965, when it was used by Harris & Co. Until 1917, North Box had controlled this area.

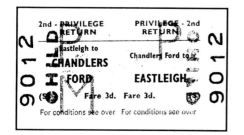

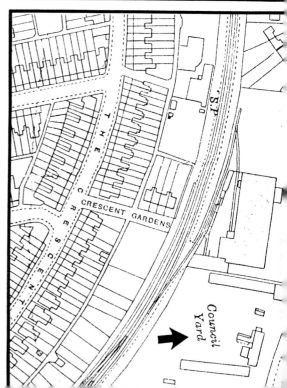

WEST OF EASTLEIGH

66. On the left is the gate on the private siding to P. M. Combes' timber yard, which was open to traffic from 1951 to 1966.   No. 34059 *Sir Archibald Sinclair* is approaching Eastleigh on 30th May 1959, hauling a Bristol (Parson Street) to Portsmouth excursion.   (L. Elsey)

**Eastleigh is also included
in the following
Middleton Press albums -**

**Woking to Southampton
Steaming through East Hants
Steaming through West Hants**

67. Rolling stock manufactured at Eastleigh was often to be seen on trial locally. A short-framed Hastings DEMU is seen on a test run to Andover, on 26th March 1957. (L. Elsey)

EASTLEIGH MARSHALLING YARDS

Until the opening of Feltham Marshalling Yard in 1921, Eastleigh was the most important marshalling point for freight trains on the LSWR. It was not only the crossing point of the main line between London and Dorchester with that between the West Country and Portsmouth, but also nearly all traffic between Portsmouth and LSWR stations was routed via Eastleigh. This was due to the heavy gradients on the Portsmouth Direct line and the Netley line.

Soon after grouping the SR diverted traffic between the Western Section and the southern half of the Central section from the Wimbledon - Norwood route to the Havant - Cosham route and introduced a daily service in each direction between Brighton and Eastleigh, calling at Chichester and Havant. Gradually more use was made of this route. Some of the considerable quantity of sugar beet produced each season in West Sussex was sent to the factories at Kidderminster and Colwick and was routed from Chichester via Eastleigh and Basingstoke. Steam coal from South Wales for the locomotive department was run on through trains from Salisbury to Chichester and sometimes Three Bridges.

As a result of upgrading the Didcot, Newbury and Southampton line for WWII traffic, direct services were put on after the war between Eastleigh and Banbury using this route. Not only sugar beet, but empty mineral wagons were regularly worked from the Chichester area to the former Great Central line via this route.

When, in the 1960's, the National Freight Train Plan was brought in, Feltham was run down and Eastleigh again became the principal marshalling yard of the Western section of the Southern Region. Through trains were introduced between Eastleigh and Bristol West Depot, Severn Tunnel Junction via Salisgury, and Bescot via Reading.

CHANDLERS FORD

68.   A down train from Eastleigh enters the small rural station which was opened when services to Salisbury commenced on 1st March 1847.   "Down" also describes trains to Fare-ham, so the designation changes at Eastleigh, reflecting the railway evolution.
(Lens of Sutton)

69.   The station master's house was more imposing than the station buildings, access to which was from the up side only.   The bridge now carries the B3043 and the platforms still exist.   (Lens of Sutton)

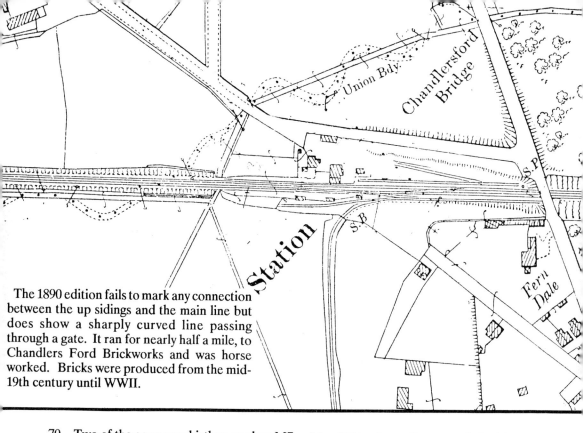

The 1890 edition fails to mark any connection between the up sidings and the main line but does show a sharply curved line passing through a gate. It ran for nearly half a mile, to Chandlers Ford Brickworks and was horse worked. Bricks were produced from the mid-19th century until WWII.

70. Two of the gang are shirtless as class M7 no. 30479 departs east, still carrying its winter snowplough. The goods yard closed on 4th May 1964. In earlier years, it had been provided with a 30 cwt. crane. The cylinder on the left is an oil tank. (D. Cullum coll.)

71. A 1957 photograph shows that the station
was electrically lit by then. The timber framed
signal box was in use until 22nd May 1969.
(H. C. Casserley)

Developments by the time of the 1909 survey
include a footbridge, a longer up siding and the
"Railway Hotel", now the "Monks Brook".

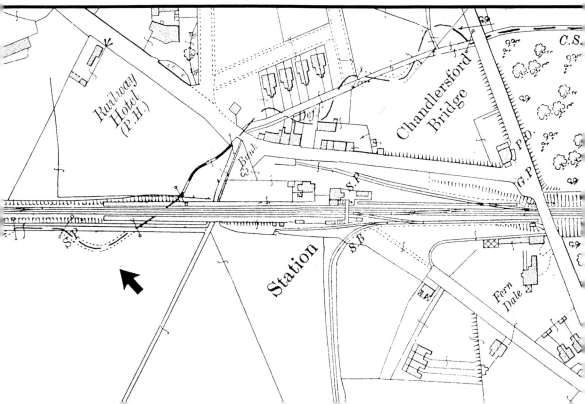

72. Passenger services were withdrawn on 5th May 1969, the day on which this photograph was taken. The crossover was removed in 1971 and the down line was taken out of use on 1st May 1972. (J. H. Bird)

73. A mystery tour from South Wales to South-east England passed through the nameless station in July 1969, no doubt adding to the mystery for some. Some freight and stone services, some empty stock and light engines together with a few unscheduled passenger trains still use the remaining single line. Some 20 to 30 movements daily are still made. (J. H. Bird)

ROMSEY

74. Points of interest in this early view are the shunting horse, the low level of the platform, the design of the verandah style awning, the coupled chimney stacks and the contrasting window styles, indicating an early extension to the original building.   A similar design was employed at Micheldever.
(National Railway Museum)

75. A later view shows the raised level of the platform and extension of the canopy.   The extent of the staff is also noteworthy.
(Lens of Sutton)

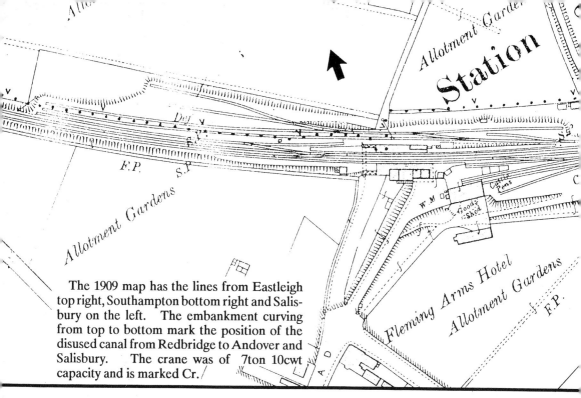

The 1909 map has the lines from Eastleigh top right, Southampton bottom right and Salisbury on the left. The embankment curving from top to bottom mark the position of the disused canal from Redbridge to Andover and Salisbury. The crane was of 7ton 10cwt capacity and is marked Cr.

76. The driver of class L12 no. 30432 looks on as parcel traffic is dealt with on 9th July 1949. The two tracks on the extreme left passed behind the up platform buildings to link six of the seven sidings with the main line, near the junction. These were used as local marshalling sidings. (H. C. Casserley)

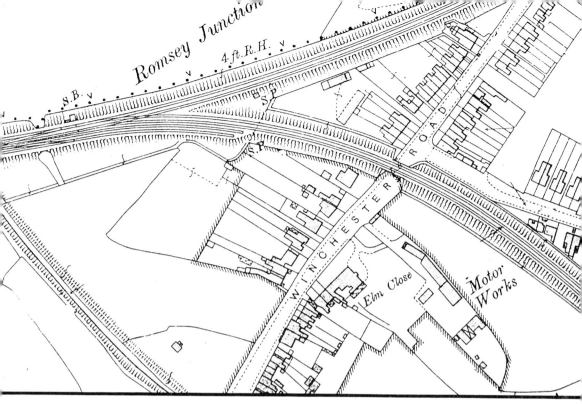

77. The building at the far end of the platform is the gents, surmounted by a water tank for locomotive purposes. At the opposite end is the staff room, with a single chimney. This 1957 view was little changed 32 years later, and even the goods shed survived, in use by a tyre supplier. (H. C. Casserley)

78. The 27-lever box closed on 17th October 1982, the signals having been converted to colour lights in 1976. The position of the box, close to the junction, is shown on the map. The box is preserved in the grounds of a nearby school. (J. Scrace)

80. The exterior condition is shown in 1981 and eight years later it had been enhanced by brick cleaning and other refurbishment. The white rail marks the edge of the weighbridge. (D. Cullum)

←

79. The position of the cattle dock and goods shed are evident, as DEMU no. 1104 arrives on 2nd May 1964. The goods yard closed on 20th July 1970. A water column can be seen at the end of the up platform - another, for freight locomotives is partly obscured by the passenger's head. (C. L. Caddy)

81. The colour light signal and route indicator, at this end of the down platform, was added in 1979 to facilitate the reversal of terminating down trains. The train is the 11.05 Exeter St. Davids to Portsmouth Harbour on 13th April 1988, a service that ceased entirely in May 1989. (J. Scrace)

London & South Western Ry.
This Ticket is issued subject to the Bye-laws
Regulations & Conditions stated in the Company's Time Tables Bills & Notices

CHANDLER'S FORD to
EASTLEIGH

Chandler's Ford   Chandlers Ford

Eastleigh   Eastleigh
3rd CLASS   (8.35)   3rd CLASS
Fare 2d   Fare 2d

BRITISH RAILWAYS (S)
ROMSEY
PLATFORM TICKET 1d.
Available ONE HOUR OF DATE ISSUE ONLY
NOT VALID IN TRAINS NOT TRANSFERABLE
To be given up when leaving Platform
FOR CONDITIONS SEE BACK.

82. The one remaining short siding was obscured by ex-LMS class 8F no. 48151 on 2nd July 1988 when it hauled a special train from Salisbury. It had run round its train and is waiting to use the crossover to the down line. (J. H. Bird)

> **Other views of trains on this part of the route are included in the Middleton Press album** *Steaming through West Hants.*

KIMBRIDGE JUNCTION

83. Looking towards Romsey from the Andover lines on 24th May 1966, we see the signal box that was in use from 21st March 1943 until 14th June 1967. Its predecessor had been on the other side of the track. Passenger services to Andover had been withdrawn on 7th September 1964. (D. Cullum)

84. A demolition train waits to run off the remaining single track on 4th August 1969, nearly five years after the line closure. Class 47 no. D1604 speeds past with an excursion from South Wales to Bognor Regis. (J. H. Bird)

85. The 13.56 from Portsmouth Harbour is passing the 14.45 from Salisbury on 20th April 1975 and is about to pass over the level crossing seen in picture no. 83. This received automatic half barriers when the signal box closed. The signal is the Dunbridge down distant, which had a slotted post as late as 1947. (J. Scrace)

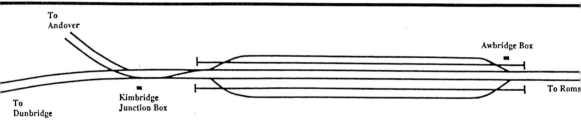

East of the junction, two goods loops were laid each side of the main line in 1943, to handle some of the increased traffic prior to the invasion of Europe. Awbridge signal box was built at the Romsey end, it being in use until 1946. The outer loops became disused in 1948 and the inner ones followed in 1952.

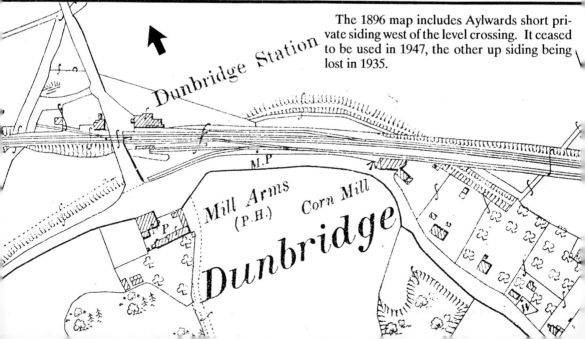

The 1896 map includes Aylwards short private siding west of the level crossing. It ceased to be used in 1947, the other up siding being lost in 1935.

MOTTISFONT
(DUNBRIDGE)

86. The station opened with the line and was endowed with a substantial house (left). The Mill Arms is in the centre and the signal box is on the right of the rough surfaced road. (Lens of Sutton)

87. The porter prepares to attend to the 2.33pm Portsmouth & Southsea to Bristol Temple Meads train, which was composed mainly of ex-LNER coaches on 13th July 1957. The 5-ton crane is partly visible. (P. Hay)

88. The goods yard was closed on 7th August 1961 and remained unused nearly 30 years later. DEMU no. 1111 arrives from Romsey on 2nd May 1964, before the introduction of yellow warning triangles and yellow ends on multiple units. (C. L. Caddy)

89. The River Dun passes under the railway to the left of the signal box and under the road just beyond the level crossing. This is the peaceful scene in 1966 - at least the station building remained intact in 1989. The roofs of the cottage style appendages to the signal box are visible. (D. Cullum)

90. Controlled barriers came into use on 22nd September 1974, their installation necessitating the repositioning of the signal box steps. They were replaced by automatic half barriers when the signal box closed on 14th November 1982. (C. Hall)

91. The name Mottisfont was applied from 16th May 1988, it having been earlier used on the first station on the Andover line. This is the unusual scene on 2nd July 1988, when dairy tankers were used to supply water to class 4 2-6-4T no. 80080 which was running from Romsey to Salisbury. (J. H. Bird)

92.   Half a mile west of Dunbridge, sidings were provided on the up side in 1943 to serve a massive U.S. Army supply depot. Lockerley signal box controlled access to them until they closed in 1949. Nearly a mile further west, the Admiralty established a large armaments depot on the down side at Dean Hill and sidings came into use in 1940. They remained connected to BR in 1989 and no. 47125 is seen leaving with 08.56 Eastleigh to Severn Tunnel Junction Speedlink service on 24th January 1986. (C. Wilson)

93.   Beyond the crossing is Dean Hill Box, which was in use from May 1940 until May 1977, when automatic half barriers were commissioned. Ex-LNER no. 4498 *Sir Nigel Gresley* runs towards Salisbury on 3rd June 1967. (J. Scrace)

DEAN

94. The imposing station house and the externally framed signal box are seen from the bridge over the small River Dun. Class 460 no. 471 stands at the down platform - no less than ten oil lamps were provided on the up platform. (Lens of Sutton)

95. Class T3 no. 557 passes the much modified signal box, sometime in the 1930s. The ornate valance had gone and the framing had been clad with weather boards. (Lens of Sutton)

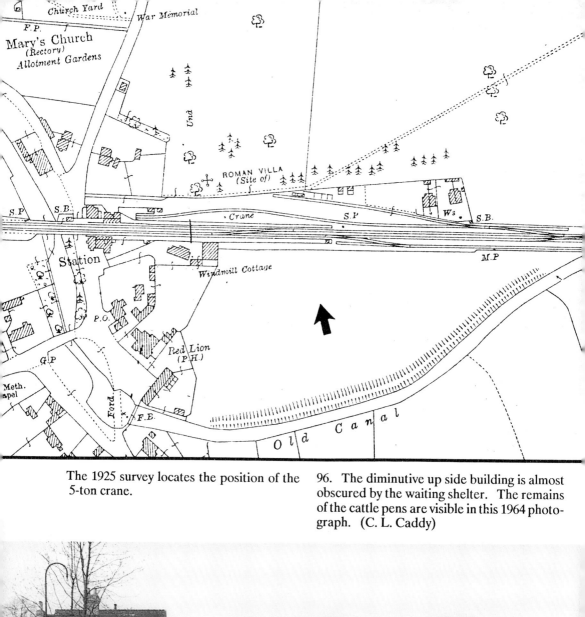

The 1925 survey locates the position of the 5-ton crane.

96. The diminutive up side building is almost obscured by the waiting shelter. The remains of the cattle pens are visible in this 1964 photograph. (C. L. Caddy)

97. The architectural style of the station was in harmony with that of the parish church of St. Mary's. The village is West Dean, East Dean being a mile down the valley. Two bicycles and no cars sufficed for passengers on 16th February 1968. (J. Scrace)

98.   Seen on the same day, the signal box remained in use until 9th September 1980, when automatic half barriers were brought into action. The up shelter and down buildings were still standing in 1989. (J. Scrace)

99. No. 56063 was heading the 9.55 Ardingly to Whatley Quarry stone empties on 14th May 1988 as they passed the two pairs of railway-built cottages and the sole remaining siding, retained by the engineers. (M. Turvey)

100. Two miles west of Dean, sidings were laid on the down side in 1972 to serve East Grimstead Quarry. For over ten years chalk was taken from it to the English China Clay's works at Quidhampton, two miles west of Salisbury, where it was processed into a slurry for use in production of white paper. Much of the finished product was sent by rail tanker to Scotland. No. 33117 passes the entrance to the quarry with the 9.32 Marchwood to Salisbury freight on 24th February 1986. In 1989, the quarry sidings were used for the storage of withdrawn 4TC sets. (A. Dasi-Sutton)

ALDERBURY JUNCTION

101. Nearly four miles west of Dean, the single line from West Moors and Downton joined on the down side, until closure of that route on 4th May 1964. The Brighton to Plymouth train speeds past the brick-built box on 21st October 1961, headed by no. 34038 *Lynton*. The box was not closed until 1st December 1970. (E. Wilmshurst)

102. Just west of the junction, two low platforms were provided for use by local railway staff and their wives. The platforms are seen in June 1964. (D. Cullum)

103.   Class 4 2-6-4Ts nos. 80152 and 80016 return east on 17th September 1966 with a rail tour run by Locomotive Preservation (Sussex) Ltd from Victoria to Salisbury. It was hauled by *Flying Scotsman* to Eastleigh via Hove. The site of the junction is now marked by the convergence of the A36 dual carriageway with the railway, as it was built on part of the trackbed of the West Moors line to bypass the village of Alderbury. (J. Scrace)

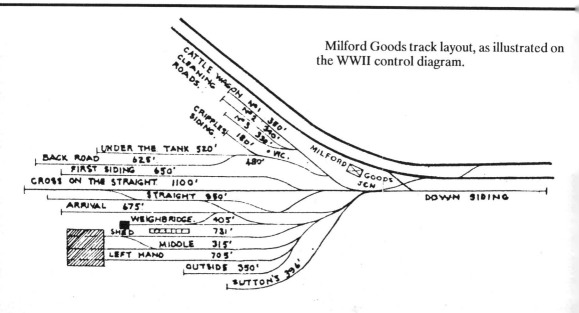

Milford Goods track layout, as illustrated on the WWII control diagram.

MILFORD GOODS

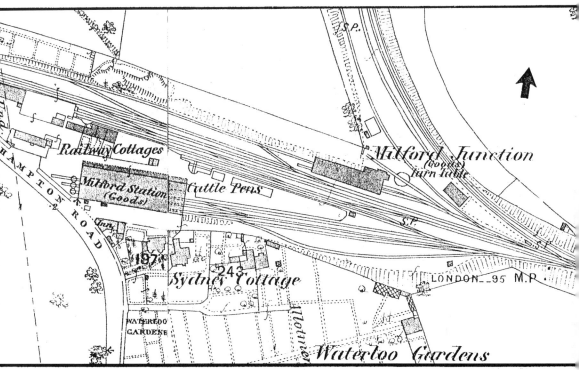

This 1881 map shows the site of the terminus that was used by passengers from 1st March 1847 until the line was extended to the Salisbury & Yeovil Railway station on 2nd May 1859. Trains from London via Andover used Milford station from 1st May 1857 but this involved an inconvenient reversal. The locomotive shed, near the turntable, was used as a store after 1859. The first train arrived on 27th January 1847, carrying 100 tons of coal, a gift to the poor of the city.

104. Some idea of the extent of the yard can be obtained as no. 34027 *Taw Valley* rounds the 12 chain curve with the Plymouth to Brighton service on 21st October 1961. Extreme left is the goods shed and to the left of the signal box is the former engine shed, by then bricked up. (E. Wilmshurst)

105. The box had an ornate double valance and a 28 lever 1895 Dutton frame. The yard closed on 21st August 1967 and the box followed on 1st January 1968. (E. Wilmshurst)

°9534

2nd - SINGLE
DUNBRIDGE
to
FARE
ROMSEY
VALID
days
For
enquire ticket
NOT TRANSFERA

In 1934, the Southern Railway Magazine described the depot thus -

The Milford Goods Station presents a scene of great activity at certain times, notably on market days, when as many as 40 wagons may be loaded during one afternoon. The yard is well able to deal with sudden influxes of traffic on its 17 roads, all of which bear names instead of the more usual numbers, due to the remaining features of the old passenger terminus equipment. It is rather unfortunate, however, that owing to the slope of the ground wagons will run out of every road except one, unless braked, so it is anything but a gravity yard. The capacious goods shed becomes a transfer shed between 10pm and 6am, wherein about 45 wagons are dealt with nightly to enable next day deliveries to be given with "smalls" between stations on the Western and the Eastern Divisions. There are a dozen coal pens for unloading coal through the bottom of trucks and special provision has been made for handling large timber, a 10-ton crane and wide loading docks assisting in the dispatch of this and similar awkward loads. The July wool traffic is always a considerable event, ten days being required to clear the effects of a sale, but apart from such exceptional times the every day work of the yard includes the sorting of about 250 vehicles, so that although Milford station may have lost some of the glory of former days it has lost none of its utility.

106.   North of Milford Junction, there is a straight length of track in the Bourne Valley before reaching a triangular junction at the approach to Fisherton Tunnel.   No. 34019 *Bideford* is running south on 14th August 1965, with cement from Westbury to Poole. (S. C. Nash)

107.   Although the earthworks gave the impression of the existence of a triangular junction, it had never been completed.   When trains from Andover were diverted to the present station in 1859, the eastern side was retained and was in use as a siding from the Milford end until 1933.   On 21st August 1981 a new single line finally completed the triangle. It was intended for use by diverted London - Southampton trains but was also found useful for other traffic and for the steam specials operated in 1988, one of which is seen at Laverstock South Junction.   (J. H. Bird)

108. Class 4 no. 75070 was in charge of an RCTS railtour from Waterloo to Southampton Docks and Fawley on 20th March 1966. In the absence of a triangle, it reversed at Salisbury and is seen taking the Romsey line, the line from Waterloo being behind the box, which closed on 17th August 1981.
(D. Fereday Glenn)

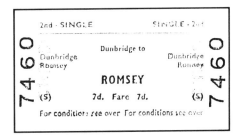

109. The 10.35 Cardiff General to Portsmouth Harbour emerges from the 443yd long Fisherton Tunnel on 3rd April 1965, headed by class 4 2-6-0 no. 76009. Surprisingly, the signal engineers named the tunnel differently - Salisbury Tunnel. (S. C. Nash)

110. The rear of the train is still in the tunnel as 2-8-0 no. 48151 passed under the modern bridge of the Salisbury ring road on 2nd July 1988. The headshunt of East Yard is on the left. (J. Petley)

SALISBURY

111.   On the right is part of the original 1859 station which was retained mainly for parcel traffic when the new buildings were erected in 1901-02.   The spacious booking hall retains much of its earlier elegance and some of the old signs have recently been restored. (Lens of Sutton)

113. No. 145 was one of Adams class 135 and is seen leaving platform 1, showing the head-code for Southampton Docks via Eastleigh. The locomotive was in traffic from 1881 until 1913. On the right is the roof of the GWR terminus. (D. Cullum coll.)

112. One platform sufficed for the first station, an up platform being added later, east of the road bridge. A down bay was also added at the London end, access to the up platform being along the bay platform and through a subway - see map. The rebuilding resulted in four through platforms and two bays. The footbridge connected the LSWR platforms with the GWR terminus, which remained in use until 12th September 1932.
(Lens of Sutton)

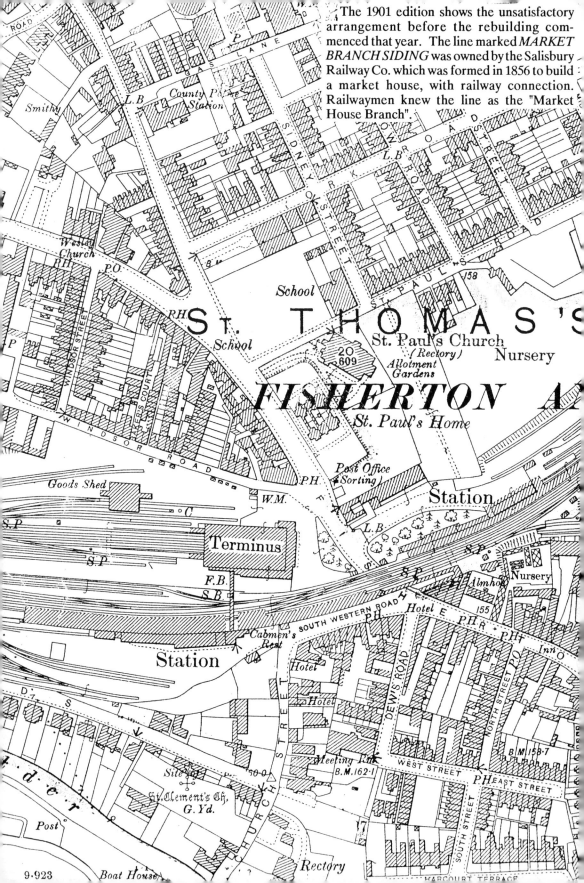

The 1901 edition shows the unsatisfactory arrangement before the rebuilding commenced that year. The line marked *MARKET BRANCH SIDING* was owned by the Salisbury Railway Co. which was formed in 1856 to build a market house, with railway connection. Railwaymen knew the line as the "Market House Branch".

St. THOMAS'S

FISHERTON A

9·923

SOUTHERN RAILWAY.
This Ticket is issued subject to the By-laws
Regulations & Conditions stated in the
Company's Time Tables Bills & Notices
Available on DAY of issue ONLY
DUNBRIDGE to
Dunbridge   Dunbridge
Salisbury   Salisbury
SALISBURY
Third Class   Third Class
Fare 1/8   Fare 1/8

1738   1738

114.   No. 34047 *Callington* leaves the same platform in August 1958, heading the Cardiff to Brighton service, which ran via Southampton Central.   The DEMU in the bay platform (no. 6) is no. 1103 and was destined for Eastleigh.   (T. Wright)

115.   A 1973 photograph confirms that the original building was still largely used for parcels.   In 1981, one of the rooms was adapted to accommodate a new signalling panel, which came into use in August of that year, replacing the two electro-pneumatic station boxes.   It eventually controlled the four routes as far as Dunbridge, Tisbury, Westbury and Grateley. (J. Scrace)

116.   DEMU no. 1130 is seen on 29th April 1982 waiting in the bay which was originally provided for the Bulford branch services.   The barrow crossing was subsequently removed in the interest of safety, as an adaquate subway exists.   (D. Cullum)

117. Until May 1988, a regular hourly occurrence on weekdays was the departure of the Cardiff to Portsmouth Harbour train behind a class 33. This is no. 33029 on 14th July 1984, complete with snowploughs. The DEMU, on the left, always departed shortly after and usually called at all stations. (A. Dasi-Sutton)

118. The 11.10 Portsmouth Harbour to Cardiff Central service waits at platform 4 on 21st April 1988 behind no. 33103. Good connections with trains on the Yeovil - Exeter line were generally available at this provincial crossroads. (J. Scrace)

119.   The Market House branch once dropped away steeply on the ground behind the Sprinter, and five carriage sidings were available by the water tank.   Class 158 air conditioned Sprinters are proposed for the route and those customers with long legs hope then for more space. (P. G. Barnes)

120. A second picture from 4th March 1989, also taken from platform 6, shows another Sprinter, no. 156471. This class certainly lives up to its name and gives Salisbury an enhanced cross country service to complement the regular Waterloo - Exeter service. (P. G. Barnes)

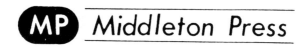

Easebourne Lane, Midhurst, West Sussex,
GU29 9AZ
Midhurst (0730) 813169

BRANCH LINES

BRANCH LINES TO MIDURST
BRANCH LINES AROUND MIDHURST
BRANCH LINES TO HORSHAM
BRANCH LINES TO ALTON
BRANCH LINE TO HAYLING
BRANCH LINE TO SOUTHWOLD
BRANCH LINE TO TENTERDEN
BRANCH LINES TO NEWPORT
BRANCH LINES TO TUNBRIDGE WELLS
BRANCH LINE TO SWANAGE
BRANCH LINES TO LONGMOOR
BRANCH LINE TO LYME REGIS
BRANCH LINE TO FAIRFORD
BRANCH LINE TO ALLHALLOWS
BRANCH LINES AROUND ASCOT
BRANCH LINES AROUND WEYMOUTH
BRANCH LINE TO HAWKHURST

SOUTH COAST RAILWAYS

BRIGHTON TO WORTHING
CHICHESTER TO PORTSMOUTH
BRIGHTON TO EASTBOURNE
RYDE TO VENTNOR
EASTBOURNE TO HASTINGS
PORTSMOUTH TO SOUTHAMPTON
SOUTHAMPTON TO BOURNEMOUTH
ASHFORD TO DOVER
BOURNEMOUTH TO WEYMOUTH

SOUTHERN MAIN LINES

WOKING TO PORTSMOUTH
HAYWARDS HEATH TO SEAFORD
EPSOM TO HORSHAM
CRAWLEY TO LITTLEHAMPTON
THREE BRIDGES TO BRIGHTON
WATERLOO TO WOKING
VICTORIA TO EAST CROYDON
TONBRIDGE TO HASTINGS
EAST CROYDON TO THREE BRIDGES
WOKING TO SOUTHAMPTON
WATERLOO TO WINDSOR
LONDON BRIDGE TO EAST CROYDON

COUNTRY RAILWAY ROUTES

BOURNEMOUTH TO EVERCREECH JNCT
READING TO GUILDFORD
WOKING TO ALTON
BATH TO EVERCREECH JUNCTION
GUILDFORD TO REDHILL
EAST KENT LIGHT RAILWAY

STEAMING THROUGH

STEAMING THROUGH KENT
STEAMING THROUGH EAST HANTS
STEAMING THROUGH SURREY
STEAMING THROUGH WEST SUSSEX
STEAMING THROUGH THE ISLE OF WIGHT
STEAMING THROUGH WEST HANTS

OTHER RAILWAY BOOKS

WAR ON THE LINE
GARRAWAY FATHER & SON
LONDON CHATHAM & DOVER RAILWAY
INDUSTRIAL RAILWAYS OF THE SOUTH
EAST

OTHER BOOKS

MIDHURST TOWN THEN & NOW
EAST GRINSTEAD THEN & NOW

MILITARY DEFENCE OF WEST SUSSEX
SUSSEX POLICE FORCES

WEST SUSSEX WATERWAYS
SURREY WATERWAYS